# MY FIRST GARDEN

Everything You Need to Know About
the Birds, Butterflies, Reptiles, and
Animals in Your Backyard

10 9 8 7 6 5 4 3 2 1

Manufactured in China, December 2021
This product conforms to CPSIA 2008

Library of Congress Cataloging-in-Publication Data is available on file.

Cover design provided by Éditions Rustica
Cover illustration by Charlène Tong

Print ISBN: 978-1-5107-6397-5
Ebook ISBN: 978-1-5107-6398-2

Bénédicte Boudassou
Illustrations by Charlène Tong
Translated by Grace McQuillan

# MY FIRST GARDEN

Everything You Need to Know About
the Birds, Butterflies, Reptiles, and
Animals in Your Backyard

Sky Pony Press
New York

# CONTENTS

# EARTHWORMS

Earthworms are among the most numerous and most useful animals on the planet! In one square yard of good garden soil, you might find as many as 250 of them. Get to know these slimy and legless animals—they are totally harmless.

## They dig and dig ...

The earthworm swallows any pieces of leaves, twigs, branches, and other plant debris it encounters while digging its underground tunnels. When this debris is on top of the soil, it will go looking for it to bring it back underground so it can digest it. This is why we often see earthworms when we're starting a compost pile in the yard.

### Compost pile?

This is what we call a pile of decomposing branches, leaves, and vegetable peelings.

## Pink, red, brown ...

You will find several kinds of earthworms in colors ranging from pink and brown to bright red. These different earthworm species live in different layers of the soil, not together. Each one has its own role in the layer of soil it is living in, so there are never any arguments between neighbors!

## Tracking earthworms

When the worm has completely digested all of the plant debris, it spits it out in little piles of dirt that look like tiny pieces of poop. Check your lawn: if you find any of these piles between the blades of grass, the lawn is healthy!

## Always cool

Since it breathes through its skin, the earthworm must always stay wet. Don't leave it on the pavement or in the street when you are finished observing it. Put it back in the ground or in the compost pile.

## Head or tail?

How can you recognize an earthworm's head? Even if you use a magnifying glass to look at it, it's not easy. The best way is to locate the part of its body that looks a bit swollen: the mouth is on this side. On the other end, the earthworm's anus pushes out the dirt it has digested.

## Earthworm enemies

Earthworms are a treat for many other animals, including hedgehogs, toads, and moles. Birds also wait eagerly at the end of rainstorms to spy even the tiniest worm. Unfortunately, humans are earthworms' greatest enemies because they pour insecticides and weed killers on the ground.

Stop using insecticides!
What am I going to eat if the insects are dead?

Yum!

Boo!

# THE EARTHWORM RESTAURANT

Yum Yum!

To welcome earthworms to your yard, invite them to dine at a restaurant they'll love. They will gulp down the food you give them and transform it into wonderful potting soil for your plants.

**1** Collect dry leaves, little branches, old stems, and wilted flowers. When your parents cut the grass, ask them for two shovelfuls of grass clippings. You can also collect vegetable peelings and egg cartons in a bucket for one week.

**2** In a corner of the yard, mark out a square 20 inches on each side and surround it with large stones. You will form your 8-inch tall compost pile in this square.

**3** Start by sprinkling over the dried leaves and pieces of small broken branches. Then add your vegetable peelings and grass clippings.

**4** Cut your egg cartons into little pieces and place these on top of the pile with some wilted flowers. Water with a fine spray and wait a few days.

**5** To activate your compost, stir it with a shovel or small garden fork.

## What happens next?

After two weeks, lift up some of the compost with your shovel. You will discover earthworms at work. Let them work and water the pile whenever the weather is very dry. The worms will end up transforming everything into potting soil that is good for your plants.

## When will they come outside?

Wait for it to rain. After the rain stops falling, you will find several earthworms on the ground. They love the humidity. Sometimes, when it rains for a long time, they also come out to save themselves from drowning. Take a close look at them you'll notice that their bodies are made up of rings that contract to help them move along.

# ROBINS, TITMICE, AND BLACKBIRDS

These three birds are easy to recognize when they come to your yard looking for something to eat. The robin has an orange breast and is always hopping along the ground. The titmouse has a yellow stomach and the top of its head is blue like its wings. The blackbird is black and in Europe it has a yellow beak. It is the largest of the three.

## Taming a robin

For several days in a row, either in the morning or at the end of the day, scrape the ground around your plants and along your hedges to turn over the leaves. Robins are curious and they will hop along next to you to see what you are doing and, more importantly, to enjoy the insects and tiny larvae you turn over with your rake.

curious!

**Fattening up**

The titmouse can swallow its own weight in insects, larvae, and caterpillars every day. What an appetite!

Hello, Mrs. Titmouse!

# Where should I place birdfeeders?

Robins and blackbirds like to eat on the ground. Take the large saucer from a ceramic pot to use as a birdfeeder and place it at the foot of a bush. It will not tip over when birds stand along the edge. Titmice prefer a birdfeeder attached to the branches of large shrubs. They will also come peck at sunflower seeds if you leave some on the windowsill.

Hello, Mr. Blackbird!

# What do they eat?

These three bird species devour insects, worms, and larvae from spring to autumn. They also like wild berries and seeds, especially in winter when there is no longer anything else to eat. Give them a mixture of seeds, in particular sunflower seeds, along with walnuts and hazelnuts that have been carefully crushed. Make sure not to give them dried fruits because these contain salt. In the winter, the birds might die of thirst!

# COLLECTING SEEDS FOR BIRDS

Grow plants that produce seeds that are easy to harvest. Then you can offer them to the birds in your yard.

**1** In early June, choose a large pot 16 inches wide and place it in the sun in a corner of your patio or yard. Fill it halfway with dirt. Water using a watering can with an upside-down spray head.

**2** Take a handful of amaranth seeds and mix them with a pinch of sand. Sprinkle these seeds on top of the dirt and cover with half an inch of dirt.

**3** Wait one or two weeks and water the seeds with a fine spray whenever the weather is dry. When the seedlings are 4 inches tall, pull out the shortest ones and keep the prettiest one. It will grow to about 3 feet tall.

**4** Keep watering all summer to keep the soil from drying out, and every two weeks add a dose of fertilizer for flowering plants to the water. Long tassels of red flowers will grow and fall down over the leaves.

## Watch them!

Birds are already living in your yard, so why not enjoy watching them? Lend them a helping hand by installing birdfeeders for the winter!

## What happens next?

In the fall, the flowers produce seeds. Cut off the tassels and hang them from a shrub's branches or shuck the seeds into the birdfeeders.

# LADYBUGS

Thanks to their black spots and red wing covers, ladybugs are very popular! They are the most beautiful beetles in the yard. Grandmothers often say that they bring good luck, but they are also well-liked because they help gardeners by devouring aphids.

## On foot or by air?

The European ladybug has wings that it uses to fly from plant to plant to find its food. The Asian ladybug does not have wings and gets around by walking. The sale of Asian ladybugs is now prohibited in some countries because they frighten native ladybugs away!

### What are auxiliary insects?

Auxiliary insects like the ladybug help gardeners fight against plant parasites.

## How are ladybugs born?

An adult female ladybug lays between 400 and 1,000 eggs and glues them under a leaf in the month of May. At first these eggs are bright yellow and shiny, then they turn black when the larvae are ready to emerge. Some stores sell ladybug eggs and larvae to put on plants with an aphid infestation.

## A real stinker!

To escape its enemies, the ladybug produces a bitter substance that smells very bad and gives it a horrible taste.

## Two plant friends

Fennel and catmint will attract ladybugs every time! If you have fennel in your yard, inspect the stems and leaves and you will probably find ladybug nymphs. In the winter, ladybugs take shelter in catmint plants because their dry and bushy foliage protects them from the cold. Don't bother them!

## A life

A ladybug can live for up to three years.

# RAISING LADYBUGS

Help plants get rid of their aphids by creating a ladybug nursery! You will be able to follow these pretty beetles' various transformations day by day.

### Beetles?

These insects have rigid outer wings called elytra that form a shell with two soft wings hidden underneath. When ladybugs fly, they open the elytra to unfold their larger wings.

**1** In June, purchase ladybug larvae in a garden store or on the Internet. They are usually sold in small boxes that contain pieces of popcorn.

**2** Examine the larvae. They are long, black or dark gray, with minuscule yellow spots and three pairs of legs. They don't look like adult ladybugs at all!

## What's an aphid?

These are small green or black insects that live in colonies and attach themselves to plant stems and leaves to suck out the sap. If there are too many aphids glued to one plant, the plant may weaken or die.

**3** Find a plant in the yard that has aphids. Carefully place the larvae underneath or just next to them using a paintbrush and a spoon. If the larvae are sold on pieces of popcorn, stick two or three pieces between two stems.

**4** Watch the larvae eat the aphids. They can eat up to 150 per day! After about 10 days, they will transform into nymphs and attach themselves to a plant for 5 or 6 days. The nymph eventually turns into an adult ladybug. At first, this ladybug is yellow, but within two hours it turns red and flies away!

## What happens next?

The adult ladybug also feeds on aphids and can eat 50 to 150 per day. When there are no more left to eat, the ladybug will migrate onto another plant in your yard or at your neighbor's house.

# LACEWINGS AND SOLITARY BEES

These insects are very useful. The lacewing certainly wins first prize in the beauty contest with its transparent wings, apple green body, and big golden eyes! And solitary bees are clever and resourceful; they always find a place to build their nests.

## A house for insects

There are many useful insects in your yard. Why not offer them a place to live? Their house should have several floors and compartments of different sizes filled with a variety of objects: small stones, leaves, dried stems, pieces of wood with holes, and hollow brick.

Draw out your house on a sheet of paper. Then, with your parents, look for the materials you need to build it. Decorate the roof and sides with flowers or paint and place it in your yard.

### Harmful garden insects

Harmful garden insects are insects that suck a plant's sap or eat its leaves, flowers, buds, and roots. They can do quite a bit of damage.

## How does it make its nest?

The solitary bee is both an architect and a mason! First it digs a hole in the ground or uses holes it finds around the yard (in walls, for example). Then it builds its nest with mud and small stones. It then cuts pieces of leaves and flower petals to line the nest and make it as cozy as possible! Finally, after laying its eggs, it fills the entrance with mud.

## What do they do for the yard?

The larvae of the beautiful lacewing are voracious eaters of aphids, mealybugs, and red spider mites! When they show up in the yard, you can be sure that these harmful garden insects will quickly disappear and no longer attack your plants.

The solitary bee feeds on nectar that it collects from flowers in the yard or garden. The orchard bee leaves its nest very early, around mid-March, to gather pollen from the flowers of fruit trees. By transporting pollen from flower to flower, this bee helps the trees' fruit develop properly.

*The fearsome lacewing larva*

# BUILDING INSECT SANCTUARIES

You can build shelters for helpful insects and place them all around the yard. This will allow them to hibernate in your yard and give them places to hide from their enemies.

**1** In late winter or autumn, after the shrubs in your yard are trimmed, collect dry forsythia and elderberry branches, reeds, and bamboo. These branches are hollow and can house many insects.

**2** Gather a few branches of the same length together and attach them at both ends with thick string to form a bundle. If you have enough branches, make several bundles.

## Hibernate?

Certain animals sleep all winter long. They are less sensitive to the cold because their body temperature decreases, and they breathe more slowly to use less energy.

**3** Find a ceramic pot and fill it with branches. Stand them up in the pot; they should stick out of the top. Make sure they are packed tightly together so they hold each other up and don't fall over.

**4** Place bundles of branches in several sections of the vegetable garden. You can hang them from posts, branches, fences, or a gate. Place the pot on the ground, propped up on a pile of stones in a corner of your flower garden.

## What happens next?

Depending on the season, lacewings and solitary bees will come to the sanctuary to make their nests, lay their eggs, or hibernate. You can sit next to your sanctuaries to observe them but leave the branch bundles and pot where they are to avoid disturbing the insects.

# BACKYARD BIODIVERSITY

The word biodiversity means "diversity of life" because bio means "life" in ancient Greek. Plants, animals, and microorganisms in the soil are all part of it and form the ecosystems that make up our environment. We also have our own role to play since we are living creatures, too!

## It is so important!

More and more insects and small mammals are disappearing from our yards, which is unfortunate because they play an important role in the ecological balance between harmful garden insects and auxiliary insects. Biodiversity preserves this balance to make the yard more like nature.

## Everyone is important!

Pretty ladybugs eat those awful plant-attacking aphids. But if aphids didn't exist, there wouldn't be any ladybugs, either! And in order to have butterflies flying around, we have to have their caterpillars feeding on leaves, even if sometimes this destroys plants.

Slugs stuff themselves on garden lettuce until they become a hedgehog's favorite meal, and all of the other insects fill the bellies of frogs that would disappear if they couldn't find this kind of food. This indispensable food chain is possible thanks to biodiversity.

# How can I promote biodiversity?

Increase the variety of plants in your yard and let a few plants like dandelions, clover, and daisies grow on their own in the grass. Bumblebees and butterflies love them! Cover the fence with climbing plants: birds looking for berries and insects will use them as houses and places to store food. You can also plant honey-producing flowers under fruit trees, at the base of hedges, and in flowerbeds. They attract pollinating insects that help plants produce fruit and seeds!

## Ecosystem?

An *ecosystem* is a community of living creatures that live in one particular place and interact with each other and with their environment—this could be a forest, pond, hot savanna, icy tundra, or . . . a garden!

# HEDGEHOGS

When a hedgehog is startled, it curls up into a ball, and if it feels attacked it will escape by scurrying away. This adorable mammal covered in spines is only awake at night, but you might see it in the early evening. It adores slugs and snails! Hedgehogs aren't usually found in North America, but they're so cute, we had to cover them! Imagine if they visited your backyard. . . .

## Inviting a hedgehog to your yard

To attract a hedgehog, place apple slices at the foot of a hedge. First, though, make sure it will be able to enter your yard through a small hole in the gate, between two bushes, or under the fence. Hedgehogs don't have very good eyesight and will usually walk along walls and fences, counting on their sense of smell to find food.

## Their favorite menu

Hedgehogs are omnivores and enjoy eating snails with the shells on, earthworms, frogs, insect larvae, June beetles, and spiders. They love fruit and wild berries, and in the fall they eat mushrooms and acorns. And if they stumble upon a few eggs that have fallen out of a nest, that's a real treat! Leave water for them to drink in the same small dish you set out for birds, and never give them milk because it will make them sick.

## A mile on foot...

When a hedgehog is very hungry, it may walk several miles in one night to visit the backyards around your neighborhood. It will look for anything it can swallow and moves in a zig-zag pattern. Hedgehogs also enjoy going for a drink in small ponds and pools whose banks are not very steep. In these places they can usually find a frog to complete their dinner!

## Are hedgehogs born with spines?

No. When it comes out of its mother's stomach, the hedgehog is of course all soft and smooth. The spines grow in two weeks and become hard very quickly. As an adult, a hedgehog has between 5,000 and 7,000 of them to protect it from its enemies.

## Warning: This animal is noisy, but in some countries, it is a protected species!

Once evening comes, it's easy to hear the hedgehog: as it zig-zags over the grass, it grunts, lets out little cries, and makes lots of noise during its meal. In France, hedgehogs are protected, which means that no one is allowed to capture them.

## Omnivore?

An *omnivore* is an animal that can eat anything.

Crunch!

# BUILDING A HEDGEHOG HOUSE

The hedgehog doesn't like being cold in the winter. If you build it a little house so it can sleep somewhere warm until springtime, it will come back to your yard every year.

**1** In order for a hedgehog to hibernate in winter, it needs a cozy house that will protect it from rain. In late September, choose a spot for your hedgehog house that will stay dry even when it rains. A woodshed is a good example.

**2** Find a few logs or big branches that are 16 inches long and arrange them in a tepee by squeezing them together at the top. Inside the tepee, there should be about 12 inches of space. Leave an opening 4 inches wide on one side.

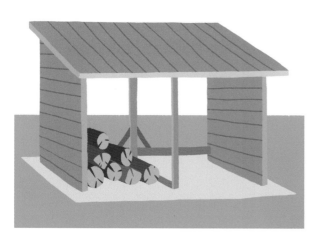

**3** Build a roof out of large dead leaves (from sycamore or maple trees, for example) by wedging them between the logs.

**4** Sprinkle smaller dead leaves around the tepee. The hedgehog will use them to finish off the inside of the house all by itself.

## What happens next?

Don't bother the hedgehog in the winter while it's sleeping. If it feels comfortable in the house you built for it, it will also let its babies live there in the spring.

# LIZARDS

Aren't lizards bizarre? They are cold-blooded animals and as fast as lightning, but they spend most of their time sleeping in the sun! Some are green, while others are gray or yellow and green. Their colors help them blend into the environment they live in.

## A varied diet

Insects, woodlice, earthworms, spiders, and mollusks are all part of a lizard's lunch. In backyards and gardens, lizards limit the insect population and work together with hedgehogs and chickens to get rid of slugs!

## What family do they belong to?

Even though they have four legs and don't look very much like snakes, lizards are part of the reptile family. Female lizards lay eggs and bury them in the ground or hide them under a big rock.

I'd love to eat a lizard!

## A passion for old walls

The little gray lizard that we often see in our backyards loves to attach itself to old walls full of holes and small walls made of dry stones. This is where it feels safest because it can use the holes to hide in and the heat from the rocks increases as the day goes on.

## As curious as a lizard!

Lizards are easily frightened, but they are still extremely curious! Whenever something unusual happens in their immediate environment, lizards come to take a look—even if it means taking a bit of a risk! If you want to attract a lizard, place a small juicy fruit like a blackberry or gooseberry in front of the pile of rocks. You will soon see it come out of its hiding place.

### Gecko

Geckos are lizards that live in tropical areas.

## Lizard enemies

Hedgehogs, stone martens, weasels, and hawks hunt lizards and swallow them whole. Shrews eat them when they are young or small in size, and cats even play with lizards before eating them! So, don't run after them and try to catch them—they have enough enemies who already do that!

# OBSERVING LIZARDS WITH BINOCULARS

On days when it's sunny and warm, take a seat in the yard and find out what lizards like to do—all without scaring them!

**1** Locate the the hottest part of your yard, near a south-facing patio, for example. It should be a spot that gets plenty of sun almost all day long. Make a small pile of about 10 stones, mixing big, flat ones 6 to 8 inches wide with rounder ones that have holes in them.

## Prey?
An animal or insect that the lizard captures to eat.

**2** This pile of stones will become a hideout spot for lizards because what they love more than anything is warming themselves in the sun near a safe place where they can quickly go and hide if they need to. Since they are easily frightened and will run away when they hear a noise or see something move, sit in a comfortable place on the other side of the patio with your binoculars focused on the pile of stones.

**3** Now you can observe the lizards without scaring them as they venture out of the pile of stones to either sunbathe on the patio or explore their surroundings on the hunt for prey to eat.

### What happens next?

If you have a camera, you can also take pictures of lizards and glue them into your wildlife reporter's notebook.

# TRIVIA

## What does the titmouse do when it sings?

1 It cheeps.
2 It clucks.
3 It chirps.
4 It cackles.

## What does the earthworm do?

**1.** It digs tunnels to use as slides.

**2.** It aerates the soil and brings oxygen into the tunnels with its many trips back and forth. Plants really appreciate this!

**3.** It eats delicious, juicy roots.

**4.** It digests small pieces of wood and leaves and transforms them into food for plant roots.

**5.** Thanks to its tunnels, it helps water seep into the ground whenever it rains a lot.

## HOW MANY SPOTS DOES A LADYBUG HAVE?

**1.** This insect has two spots when it is young, then 3, 4, 5, 6, and 7 spots as it grows up.

**2.** The ladybug with the most spots is the leader. The rest only have two spots.

**3.** Ladybugs may have different numbers of spots depending on their species.

## Where does the hedgehog hide?

1. Under your quilt to keep warm.
2. In shoes you leave outside.
3. Under piles of dried leaves next to hedges.

Answer: 3. It likes to hide in hedges and especially under a big pile of dried leaves that it can use as a nest in winter. Ask your parents not to burn any piles of leaves because this will scare hedgehogs away and kill any baby hedgehogs that might be in the nest.

## What do lacewings and bees like best?

1. Flowers.
2. Candy.
3. Insecticide.

Answer: 1. Adult lacewings and bees like flowers and feed on their pollen and nectar.

Yum! I'd love to have a little feast of ladybugs, earthworms, and lacewings, with a few birds' eggs and lizards for dessert!

## Why does the lizard lose its tail?

1. Because it is too heavy.

2. Because it often forgets about it and gets it stuck between stones.

3. Because losing its tail allows the lizard to escape when it gets caught by a predator.

Answer: 3. Lizards can slip between stones very quickly and their enemies usually only have time to grab them by their tails. The tail breaks off and the lizard is saved! Its tail grows back later, but if it loses it a second time, it might die.

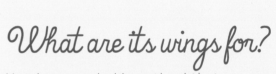

# EARWIGS

Earwigs can be frightening with their large pincers and the way they quickly run away when someone disturbs them, but they are nevertheless very useful insects that are kind to gardeners and nasty to caterpillars and aphids! Get to know them better and offer them a place to live.

## Why the name?

The earwig got its French name, *le perce-oreille*, because it was often found inside overripe peach or apricot pits. The two halves of these fruits look like ears, or *oreilles*. But don't worry. You can take a nap on the grass if you want. An earwig may come and tickle you, but it won't go in your ear. It can't even pinch you because it isn't strong enough!

### Forficula

This is the earwig's other name.

## What are its wings for?

You have probably noticed that earwigs run around on plants and that when they slip, they fall off. They are in fact able to fly, but only rarely will they unfold their little wings. Instead they use them to glide between leaves when they are perched in a tree. The rest of the time, they prefer traveling on foot!

It's gliding!

# Why is it important?

Even though it sometimes eats fruit that is very ripe, the earwig is a useful garden insect because it prefers to feed on aphids, caterpillars, and other pests that it finds on fruit trees and vegetables.

When it does eat a flower, it always waits until the flower has wilted. It will often hide inside the petals during the day and come out at night to eat the aphids clinging to the stem. It also sleeps inside heads of lettuce during the day because it doesn't like staying in the sun and wants to be there when the aphids arrive.

## Migrate?

To move or go somewhere else. Like many other animals, insects change location when they can no longer find enough food in one place.

## Let them eat

If one corner of your yard is overflowing with earwigs, this could also indicate the presence of a large number of harmful garden insects. Let nature take care of things for a few days and everything should go back to normal. After their feast, the earwigs will migrate to look for another restaurant!

# BUILDING AN EARWIG SHELTER

The earwig needs to protect itself from the sun so it doesn't fry like a sausage when it's hot outside! Give it somewhere to hide and sleep during the day.

Zzz ...

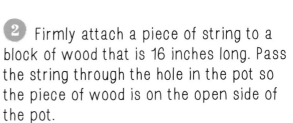

**1** Find a ceramic pot 6 inches in diameter and wash it off with a brush and some water.

**2** Firmly attach a piece of string to a block of wood that is 16 inches long. Pass the string through the hole in the pot so the piece of wood is on the open side of the pot.

I'm going to hide!

**3** Gather some dried leaves and moss from your yard. You can also use straw if you have any. Put all of this in the pot and press it down a little bit. Pull on the string so the piece of wood lies across the top of the pot. This will hold everything inside.

**4** Tie the string to the trunk of a fruit tree or on one of the lower branches.

### What happens next?

Earwigs will hide in the pot during the day. Move the pot to a different tree every month

# SQUIRRELS

This little mammal looks like a stuffed animal because of its soft fur, but it won't let you get too close. This is probably a good thing because it has long claws and pointy teeth for cracking the walnuts, hazelnuts, and acorns it loves to eat.

## Protect them

If you have a cat, make sure it doesn't run after the squirrels in your yard.
If a squirrel feels in danger, it will move to find another nest, especially if it is a female with little babies.

## A good size

The tiny African ground squirrel is barely 6 inches tall, while the black giant squirrel can reach almost 3 feet! The red squirrel in Europe measures about 8 inches tall.

## A strange-looking pinecone!

Do you know how to recognize a pinecone that a squirrel has nibbled on? There is nothing left except the core and a tiny little cap all the way at the top! The squirrel uses its front teeth to pull off the pinecone scales as it turns it around to find the seeds hidden inside.

## What kinds of trees attract squirrels?

You might be lucky enough to have a squirrel living in your yard if you have certain trees and bushes growing there. The hornbeam and the oak tree are the squirrel's favorites for building its nests. And to eat, it will gladly gather nuts from a hazel tree. Squirrels are also drawn to pine trees because their large size makes squirrels feel protected inside them. Pine trees offer squirrels a lookout spot that is out of harm's way and pinecones also make excellent squirrel food.

## Where do squirrels hide in winter?

When it can't find a hole in a tree, the squirrel builds itself several nests called dreys. It gathers twigs, moss, and leaves to form a large ball that sits high up in the tree branches. The male and female take turns occupying these cozy nests, then the female lives in one alone with her babies.

### Shush!

Squirrels hear everything. If you want to see one, don't make any noise.

# FEEDING SQUIRRELS

If you give squirrels something to eat, they will get used to coming to your yard quite often. This will give you a chance to get a closer look at them.

Mammal?

A mammal is an animal that carries its babies in its stomach and feeds them its milk after they are born.

Squirrels start storing food before the winter months. They don't hibernate during the cold season, but they do sleep a lot. Since they do not eat as much food during this time, they hide some away to enjoy a nice meal at the end of winter. But when they leave their nests in the spring, they often forget where their hiding places are! Give squirrels a little help in the fall, winter, and spring when they are very hungry.

**1** In spring and fall, place hazelnuts, walnuts, acorns, and pine cones in a large ceramic saucer under a tree in your yard. Also throw in some whole peanuts (unsalted and unshelled) if you find any at the store.

**2** In the fall, place rosehips or blackberries from your hedges in another saucer with some mushrooms. If it rains, empty the water from the saucers and change the food.

## What happens next?

When the weather gets very cold, you can stop giving food to the squirrel because it will not come out of its nest. But as the temperature starts to warm up, you can start putting out seeds, walnuts, and hazelnuts again. It will find very little to eat in nature at this time of year and will get into the habit of coming to see what you've left in the saucer.

# FROGS AND TOADS

They sing by croaking and are long jump champions! These funny amphibious animals with slimy skin live near ponds and pools of water. In just a few months, they pass from the egg stage to a legless tadpole stage before becoming adults. Incredible!

## Strange babies

Tadpoles emerge from frog eggs and look like fish because of their tails and huge heads. They live in water, but in just a few weeks their hind legs start to grow. Then come the front legs! Their transformation is complete once the tail disappears. Then they can jump out of the water, sit on pond plants, and hide in the grass.

## Mosquito hunt

Dragonflies catch mosquitoes and are very helpful around bodies of water where mosquitoes breed. To attract dragonflies and frogs to your yard, add a small jet of bubbling water or a waterfall with a pump to your pond. They prefer moving water.

## Frog or toad?

Frogs are not female toads—they are two different species. In fact, there are at least four different species of frogs that can be found in yards, and just as many different species of toads.

## Where did they go?

Observe the pond in winter. You won't see any frogs or toads because they all go into hiding before the first cold days to hibernate. Do you know where they go? Some dig a hole right in the ground—under a large rock, for example. Others burrow under tree roots or into the deep sludge of the pond to escape the ice. They will come out of their hiding places in March.

## Two ways to breathe

Amphibians have an interesting feature: they breathe with their skin and with their lungs. Their skin must always stay moist (like an earthworm's skin) because if it dries out, the animal will suffocate. How horrible!

# BUILDING A POND

Ponds attract all kinds of animals that come to drink and reproduce in the water. They are always very lively places where frogs enjoy making friends and singing!

**Amphibians?**

These are animals that live both in water and on land.

To create this pond, get some help from an adult.

**1** In a quiet area of your yard that is partly shady, dig a round hole 2 yards wide and 16 inches deep. Ask for help if the ground is hard. Keep the dirt you dig up and place it around the sides.

**2** Spread out a plastic tarp along the bottom and sides of the hole. Cover it with 4 inches of dirt and use the rest of the dirt to hide the edges of the hole by forming gently sloping banks.

**4** Now fill your pond with water using a small hose nozzle so you don't make any deep holes in the dirt or stir it up. When the water reaches the edges, stop filling.

**3** Plant three small rush plants in the bottom of the hole along with two pots of marsh marigold or common cottongrass in a different spot near the edge of the pond.

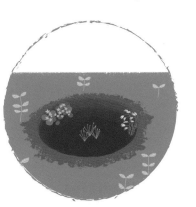

### What happens next?

Your pond is ready to welcome frogs and toads! They will sense the presence of water from far away and happily move in.

# TRY THIS!

## The wildlife reporter

Become a backyard journalist! Keep track of what happens in your yard during the summer and write everything down. It's so much fun!

**1** Begin by buying a spiral notebook and a pen that you can attach to the notebook with a string. Make sure you always have these items with you when you go out in the yard.

**3** If you don't know its name, draw it and then show the drawing to your parents. You can also look in books.

**2** Whenever you see an animal or insect, make a note in your notebook. Describe it in detail if you have time to look at it: its name, color, where it is, what it's doing, what it's eating.

**4** You can collect extra details about animals that don't run away when you come close: measure hedgehogs, earthworms, caterpillars, snails, and slugs.

**6** Follow caterpillars and observe which plants they are located on. Also make a note of butterfly color, size, and how many you see. If you continue on this treasure hunt, you will probably discover eggs and chrysalides!

**5** Make a note of what the birds are eating and glue sample seeds into your notebook or draw them. This will help you find out what each bird species in your yard likes to eat.

Don't touch the hedgehog when you measure it. Trace a line behind it and another just in front of its nose before it curls up in a ball. Then measure the distance between the lines.

# ANTS

Do you like summer camps? Ants live in camps all year long, but they're not really on vacation because they're working the whole time! They are also multi-talented and have an astonishing sense of direction.

## Ant rules of the road

You can try to make a line of ants change direction by placing an obstacle in their path, but they will just climb over it and continue on their way! If, however, you place a small pile of sugar 8 inches from their path, they will make a detour to pick some up. You will notice that there are always two lines of ants, each one going in a different direction. When they run into each other, they touch each other's antennae to give each other information. It's not just to say hello!

Ants always come back to their anthill, even if they have traveled far to look for food. They never get lost.

They may eat dead butterflies.

In winter, ants plug up the entrances to the anthill and go to sleep nestled against each other. They wake up when they feel the warmth of the sun in springtime.

## Who likes ants?

No one *really* likes them, but some ants like the red wood ant are very helpful because they feed on aphids, caterpillars, worms, and other pests. But black ants are friends with aphids and eat a sugary substance called honeydew that aphids produce. Since they like honeydew so much, black ants keep aphids near the anthill. Gardeners don't like this very much!

## Teeny tiny, but very old!

If they are not eaten up by other animals like hedgehogs, ants can live for several years. Garden ants are good at hiding and build their anthill in the ground.

# MOVING AN ANTHILL

Ants may bite your legs and tickle you when you lie down in the grass, especially if you are lying close to an anthill! Help them move to a new place so you can play without being bothered by them.

**1** Take a look at your lawn. When you see several ants walking past each other, follow them. One line is going to look for food and the other is bringing food back to the anthill. This will help you find the anthill entrance.

**2** To remove the anthill from the grass and transfer it somewhere else where it won't be a nuisance to anyone, use a ceramic pot 12 inches in diameter. Fill it with dirt from your yard and some sphagnum moss, mix together, then add some more moss.

**3** Cover the pot with a piece of wide garden mesh and attach it to the top of the pot with some string. Sprinkle with a little water.

**4** One morning when the weather is sunny and warm, turn the pot over on top of the entrance to the anthill. The ants will quickly colonize the pot.

**5** Wait three days to make sure the entire colony and the queen are in the pot. Now place the pot on the edge of the yard or somewhere else in nature!

**Sphagnum moss?**

This is a material used in potting soil that can retain water. When it gets wet, it swells up to hold the liquid.

**What happens next?**

Plug up the old entrance hole with dirt and tamp it down.

# TRIVIA

## What is its tail for?

**1.** Keeping it warm in winter.

**2.** Hiding when it feels like it is being watched.

**3.** To help it balance as it jumps from branch to branch.

*Answer: 1, 2, 3. All of these answers are correct! The squirrel's tail is extremely useful and is as long as its body.*

## I have big eyes on my wings. Why?

**1.** To frighten my enemies.

**2.** To see flowers more easily.

**3.** To look handsome so I can attract female butterflies.

*Answer: 1. On each pair of its wings, the peacock butterfly has two large circles that look like eyes to frighten predators. When it feels in danger, it beats its wings very quickly and makes its eyes look alive!*

## What are the earwig's pincers for?

**1** Biting the fingers of children who bother it.

**2** Tickling plants.

**3** Pinching creatures that want to eat it.

**4** Knitting when it gets bored.

*Answer: 3. Earwigs' pincers are a defense weapon against predators. But birds, lizards, and shrews don't care and will eat them all the same!*

## Why is it drooling?

1. It is always thirsty.
2. It has rabies.
3. It is making the ground wet so it can move forward without hurting itself.

*Answer: 3. Because snails move by crawling along the ground, they produce slime so they can slide more easily on all kinds of surfaces without getting injured. This slime is called mucus.*

# WHAT IS A FLYING ANT?

1. An ant that is trying to reproduce.
2. An ant that lives in trees.
3. An ant that is tired of walking.

*Answer: 1. Certain ants have wings during the reproductive period between June and September. Once they have mated, the males die and the females lose their wings to become queens and create new colonies.*

## Why does the midwife toad keep its eggs on its back?

1. To eat them when it gets hungry.
2. To protect them from predators.
3. It has no idea that the eggs are stuck to its skin.

*Answer: 2. The midwife toad is a very attentive dad: when the female lays her eggs, the male coils the strings of big yellow eggs on his back to protect them from all of the creatures that want to eat them. He removes them from his back when the tadpoles emerge in summer.*

# SNAILS

These gastropods are a gardener's nightmare because they devour young plants in flowerbeds and vegetable gardens! But their retracting tentacles and pretty shells make them truly irresistible. Get to know them and protect your plants from their appetite.

## Gastropod?

Snails move on their stomachs (*gastro*) thanks to their very muscular feet (*pod*).

## Shell story

A snail keeps its shell all its life. The shell is made of slime called mucus that hardens as it dries and, little by little, enlarges the shell. It is attached to the snail's body and when the weather is dry, for example, the snail can even hide inside it for long periods of time. The snail closes the shell door with a layer of mucus.

## Bubbles and bubbles . . .

To ward off its enemies, the snail makes bubbles. It makes so many that eventually it is covered in them. It does this hoping to hide or appear less appetizing to whatever creature wants to eat it!

## How can I keep them from eating my plants?

Snails have tremendous appetites, and when several of them arrive on the same plant, they often devour the whole thing. To keep this from happening, you have to block their path: surround the plants with hemp or flax seeds and add eagle fern leaves cut into tiny pieces. Snails and slugs hate all of these things! The hungry creatures won't come back as long as you maintain a fairly thick layer of this mulch.

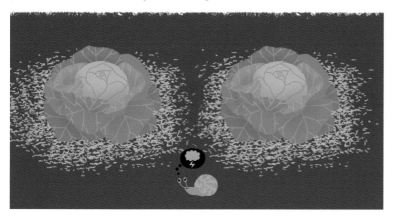

## Teeth!

Listen to a snail eat and you will notice that it's making noise . . . because it has teeth! Its tongue, called a radula, is covered with hundreds of little teeth that cut and grind up plants.

### Hermaphrodites?

This is the name given to animals that have both male and female characteristics. *All* snails can lay eggs and have babies!

# RAISING SNAILS

Discover how snails live and where they like to hide. This way you will know how to spot them in your yard and where to locate their eggs. Then it will be easier for you to catch them and bring them somewhere else.

**1** After it rains, look under leaves, the rims of pots, and along the edges of your yard until you find three or four snails. Pick them up.

**2** Pour 4 inches of dirt into a terrarium or a large, empty aquarium placed in the shade. Place four or five lettuce leaves on top of the dirt off to one side.

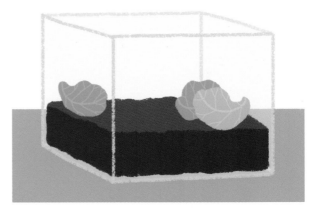

**3** Place your snails in the terrarium and cover it with a lid. This lid should have lots of tiny holes to allow air to pass through. Make sure the snails always have something to eat by adding soft lettuce leaves. Water from time to time to keep the dirt cool and the leaves damp.

**What happens next?**
Now release all of your snails back into nature. They have certainly earned their freedom!

**4** Your snails will mate because they are hermaphrodites. After mating they will dig a 2-inch hole to lay their eggs, which look like tiny white balls. You can look at the eggs, but then you should cover the hole to avoid disturbing them.

**5** The baby snails will be born after two to four weeks. When they come out of the ground, their shell is still transparent. Take a look at their tentacles: the larger ones hold up the eyes, and the smaller ones are used as antennae to sense where they are going and what they are touching.

# BUTTERFLIES

Butterflies are essential in any yard, so you should protect them! By taking part in flower pollination, they help plants produce seeds, legumes, and fruit. Unfortunately, today there are fewer and fewer butterflies because of insecticides.

## Pollination?

By transporting pollen from flower to flower, like bees do, butterflies ensure plant pollination and flower fertilization.

## From a caterpillar to a butterfly

The butterfly lays its eggs on a plant. Out of these eggs come caterpillars that snack on plants before each one transforms into a chrysalis, which is a kind of hard shell. A butterfly will emerge from each chrysalis and will gather flower nectar.

## With a straw!

Butterflies' long trunks are like straws that unroll to search for nectar deep inside flowers. This is very practical, especially when flowers have a funnel shape.

## Which caterpillar for which butterfly?

Caterpillars are crafty and never have the same coloring as the butterflies they turn into! The plump monarch caterpillar has yellow, white, and black stripes. The common blue caterpillar is green with thin yellow stripes, and the Old World swallowtail caterpillar has stripes and spots on a bright green body even though the butterfly it becomes has white and black wings.

## Gathering nectar

Attract butterflies by sowing the seeds of their favorite flowers. Buy cosmos seeds—butterflies love sitting on top of these flowers—as well as seeds for chamomile, cornflower, and pincushion plants they can collect nectar from. Sow the seeds on a sunny day after hoeing and raking the dirt. A little pinch of seeds is enough. Just sprinkle a little soil on top and water with a gentle spray. If you'd like to attract butterflies to your balcony, you can plant some lavender in a pot.

## Do butterflies drink when they are hot?

Yes, they do need to drink, and a drop of water is more than enough for them. During hot and dry summers, build a butterfly drinking station using a saucer filled with sand and water. The water level should not be higher than the sand or the butterflies will drown.

# OBSERVING PEACOCK BUTTERFLIES

If you want the chance to be there when the caterpillar transforms and when the butterfly comes out of its chrysalis, do this experiment at home. You will need a cardboard box and a clear container.

**1** Put on gloves and go looking for nettles. If you don't have any in your yard, you might find some in a rural area and along roads and trails. Under the nettle's leaves between May and September, you will see eggs or black and hairy caterpillars. Don't worry—they don't bite.

**2** Cut a few nettles with caterpillars on them. Put them in a box. Carry this cargo carefully.

**3** Place the nettles in a glass of water inside a terrarium or a large, empty aquarium with a lid. A caterpillar will typically eat a lot then stop and attach itself to a stem or the bottom of the lid to transform into a chrysalis. Watch the caterpillars as they do this. It should last one or two days.

**4** After two weeks, the chrysalis opens and releases the adult butterfly that is known as the imago. This birth lasts around 15 minutes. It's magical!

## What happens next?

Release the butterfly in your yard. If the weather is already starting to cool down, the butterfly will hibernate in your garage or a dark place in your yard like a hollow tree or shed.

# INDEX